Frances Lincoln Ltd
4 Torriano Mews
Torriano Avenue
London NW5 2RZ
www.franceslincoln.com

The Imitation of Christ
Copyright © Frances Lincoln Ltd 2004
All illustrations reproduced by kind permission of
The British Library © The British Library Board 2004.

First Frances Lincoln edition 2004

British Library Cataloguing in Publication Data
A catalogue record for this work is available from
The British Library

ISBN 0-7112-2087-5

Set in Baker Signet

Printed in Singapore

1 3 5 7 9 8 6 4 2

The Imitation of Christ

THOMAS À KEMPIS

EXTRACTS CHOSEN FROM RICHARD CHALLONER'S 1737 TRANSLATION

ILLUSTRATED WITH ILLUMINATED MANUSCRIPTS

FROM THE BRITISH LIBRARY

FRANCES LINCOLN

THOMAS À KEMPIS AND *THE IMITATION OF CHRIST*

The Imitation of Christ is a true classic of Christian spirituality, a jewel of the Middle Ages which has guided and inspired Christians of every generation over the last 600 years. Yet a modern reader opening its pages may well be put off both by the style and the content of Thomas à Kempis' spiritual reflections. Other-worldly, penitential, detached from real life, they seem distant and in some ways alien both to modern sensibilities and to the approach of contemporary Christian writers. Further reflection and closer inspection will reveal a more positive and perennial message but, as with many spiritual writers from another age, we need first of all to set Thomas' writings in the historical context of his own world and life experience. The same might be said of the writings of St Theresa of Lisieux, whose flowery, devotional language masks a deep search for and response to the mystery of God.

Thomas à Kempis was a leading member of a powerful, late-medieval spiritual movement called the Devotio Moderna, which was centred in Holland. The purpose of the movement was to rekindle the enthusiasm and practical way of life practised by the early Christian communities of Jerusalem. Members of the movement, who were known as Brothers and Sisters of the Common Life, lived lives of poverty, chastity, and obedience, some in their own homes and some in communities. They earned their living by the labour of their hands and all their earnings were placed in a common fund. There were two branches of this movement, one lay and one clerical, the latter called the Canons Regular of Windesheim. Relations between the two were close and the fundamental purpose common to both was to apply the Gospel in a radical but practical way to daily life and to bridge the gap between established religious orders and the demands of existence in the world outside.

Thomas à Kempis was born in 1379/80 into a family of artisans living in Kempen, in Holland. He followed his older brother into the 'new devotion' movement and joined the Brothers and Sisters of the Common Life at Deventer. There he became expert in transcribing manuscripts, and in 1399 he was admitted into the recently founded Canons Regular of Windesheim and was later ordained priest and twice elected subprior of the community, as well as acting as procurator for a period. He remained in this community until his death in 1471 and his various spiritual writings reflect his experience as an active and devoted member of this religious family. The most famous of these writings is *The Imitation of Christ*, which rapidly gained a wide circulation and deep respect amongst both lay and religious readers – a reputation which has lasted over the centuries both in the Catholic Church and in the broader Christian world.

At the heart of *The Imitation of Christ* lies a passionate concern for the love of Jesus Christ manifested in his words and actions and above all, in his redemptive Passion and death. The writer wishes to impart his driving desire to become a true disciple of Christ by imitating Christ's universal love and, in so doing, to deepen the disciple's spiritual understanding of Christ's redemption. At the same time, this very progress lays bare the weaknesses and sinfulness of the disciple and so guides him to embrace a life of penance and self-denial, not for its own sake or out of misguided masochism, but in order to follow more fully in the way of the cross of Christ's Passion and redemptive death.

Like all great spiritual writers, Thomas à Kempis is acutely aware of the vagaries of the human heart and the fragmented focus of human desires, and his constant concern is to direct the heart and desires of the disciple towards the reality and the love of God. This process of purification, which is both long and painful, has a double goal: to set the soul in the real world of eternal life and to strengthen the life of charity towards one's neighbour. It also provides the key to human conduct in worldly affairs, for it maintains the right scale of values, with God and Christ constantly at the centre, and so enables the individual to act in this world with the perspective of eternity.

Naturally the language and the outlook of *The Imitation of Christ* is set in a medieval world view, but Thomas à Kempis' fundamental message and teaching is authentically that of the Gospel – and if this appears at times stark and uncompromising, it may provide a healthy challenge to our modern sensibilities.

Father David Morland,
Benedictine monk

BOOK I

Useful Admonitions for a Spiritual Life

He that followeth me, walketh not in darkness, saith Our Lord. These are the words of Christ, by which we are admonished, that we must imitate His life and manners, if we would be truly enlightened, and delivered from all blindness of heart.

Let it then be our chief study to meditate on the life of Jesus Christ.

Of the Imitation of Christ, and the Contempt of All the Vanities of the World
Book I, chapter I

T he resolutions of the just depend on
the grace of God, rather than on their
own wisdom; and in Him they always put
their trust, whatever they take in hands:
For man proposes, but God disposes,
nor is the way of man in his own hands.

Of the Exercises of a Good Religious Person
Book 1, chapter 19

In festo sancte barbare virginis et martyris. Oracio.

E Xaudi nos deus salutaris noster ut sicut de beate barbare virginis tue festiuitate gaudemus: ita pie deuotionis erudiamur affectu

Per dominum. Lectio prima.

B arbara uero in ciuitate orta filia dioscori nobilis sed pagani propter nimiam pulchritudinem a patre suo in turri forti et eminenti collocatur. Jubet autem turris fieri constituit ut ibi barbara se lau

A joyful going abroad often brings
forth a sorrowful coming home;
and a merry evening makes a sad morning.
So all carnal joys enter pleasantly
but in the end bring remorse and death.

Of the Love of Solitude and Silence
Book I, chapter 20

W hy art thou troubled because things do not succeed with thee according to thy will and desire? Who is there that has all things according to his will? Neither I, nor thou, nor any man upon earth.

There is no man in the world without some trouble or affliction, though he be a king or a pope.

Of the Consideration of the Misery of Man
Book I, chapter 22

Very quickly must thou be gone from hence, see then how matters stand with thee; a man is here today and tomorrow he is vanished.

And when he is taken away from the sight he is quickly also out of mind.

Of the Thoughts of Death
Book I, chapter 23

Keep thyself as a pilgrim, and a stranger upon earth, to whom the affairs of this world do not in the least belong.

Keep thy heart free and raised upwards to God, because thou hast not here a lasting abode.

Of the Thoughts of Death
Book I, chapter 23

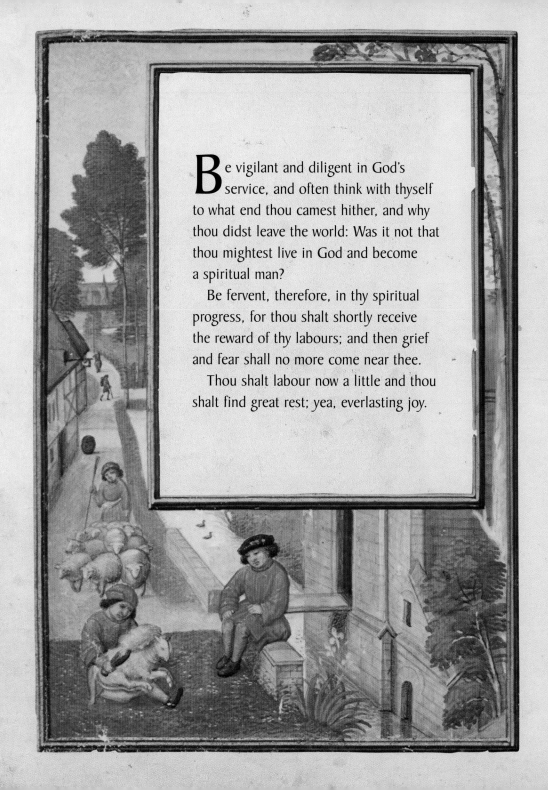

Be vigilant and diligent in God's service, and often think with thyself to what end thou camest hither, and why thou didst leave the world: Was it not that thou mightest live in God and become a spiritual man?

Be fervent, therefore, in thy spiritual progress, for thou shalt shortly receive the reward of thy labours; and then grief and fear shall no more come near thee.

Thou shalt labour now a little and thou shalt find great rest; yea, everlasting joy.

If thou continue faithful and fervent in working, God will doubtless be faithful and liberal in rewarding.

Thou must preserve a good and firm hope of winning the victory; but must not think thyself secure, lest thou grow negligent or proud.

Of the Fervent Amendment of Our Whole Life
Book I, chapter 25

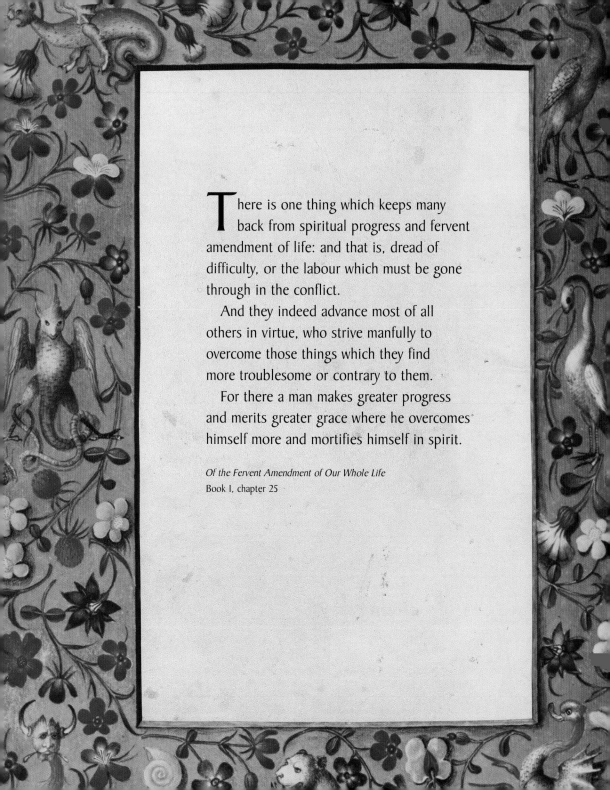

There is one thing which keeps many back from spiritual progress and fervent amendment of life: and that is, dread of difficulty, or the labour which must be gone through in the conflict.

And they indeed advance most of all others in virtue, who strive manfully to overcome those things which they find more troublesome or contrary to them.

For there a man makes greater progress and merits greater grace where he overcomes himself more and mortifies himself in spirit.

Of the Fervent Amendment of Our Whole Life
Book I, chapter 25

Oh, that we had nothing else to do but to praise the Lord our God with our whole heart and mouth!

Oh, that thou didst never want to eat, nor drink, nor sleep, but couldst always praise God and be employed solely in spiritual exercises!

Thou wouldst then be much more happy than now whilst thou art under the necessity of serving the flesh.

Would there were no such necessities, but only the spiritual refreshments of the soul, which, alas, we taste too seldom.

Of the Fervent Amendment of Our Whole Life
Book I, chapter 25

PETRVS PRVSINVS PINXIT

BOOK II

Admonitions Concerning Interior Things

Christ was also in this world despised by men, and in His greatest necessity forsaken by His acquaintance and friends in the midst of reproaches.

Christ would suffer and be despised, and dost thou dare to complain of anyone?

Christ had adversaries and backbiters, and wouldst thou have all to be thy friends and benefactors?

Whence shall thy patience be crowned if thou meet with no adversity?

If thou wilt suffer no opposition, how wilt thou be a friend of Christ?

Suffer with Christ and for Christ if thou desirest to reign with Christ.

Of Interior Conversation
Book 2, chapter 1

It is no great thing to be able to converse with them that are good and meek, for this is naturally pleasing to all. And everyone would willingly have peace and love those best that agree with them.

But to live peaceably with those that are harsh and perverse, or disorderly, or such as oppose us, is a great grace, and highly commendable and manly.

Of a Good Peaceable Man
Book 2, chapter 3

MISERICORDE

CLEMESE

IVNIQVE VOVLOIE DES PRINCES

LE GRANT PASTEVR

PAIX

DISCORDE

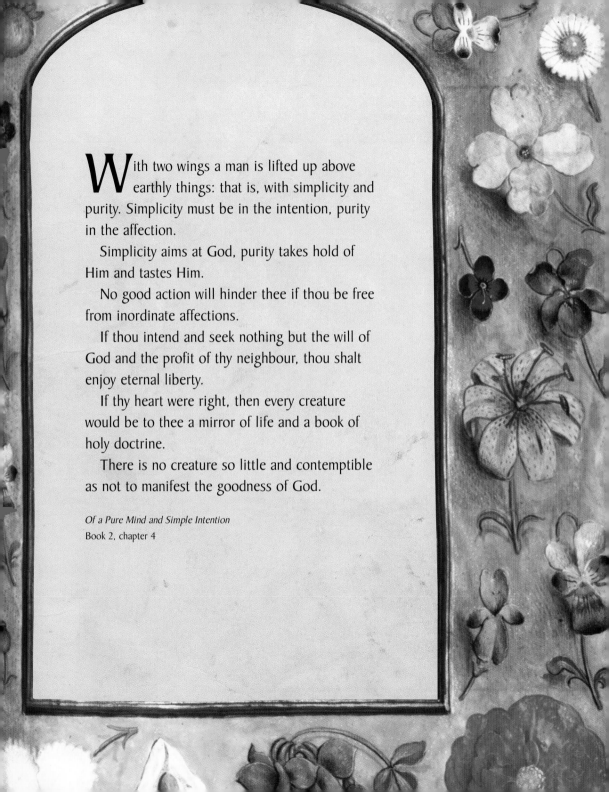

With two wings a man is lifted up above earthly things: that is, with simplicity and purity. Simplicity must be in the intention, purity in the affection.

Simplicity aims at God, purity takes hold of Him and tastes Him.

No good action will hinder thee if thou be free from inordinate affections.

If thou intend and seek nothing but the will of God and the profit of thy neighbour, thou shalt enjoy eternal liberty.

If thy heart were right, then every creature would be to thee a mirror of life and a book of holy doctrine.

There is no creature so little and contemptible as not to manifest the goodness of God.

Of a Pure Mind and Simple Intention
Book 2, chapter 4

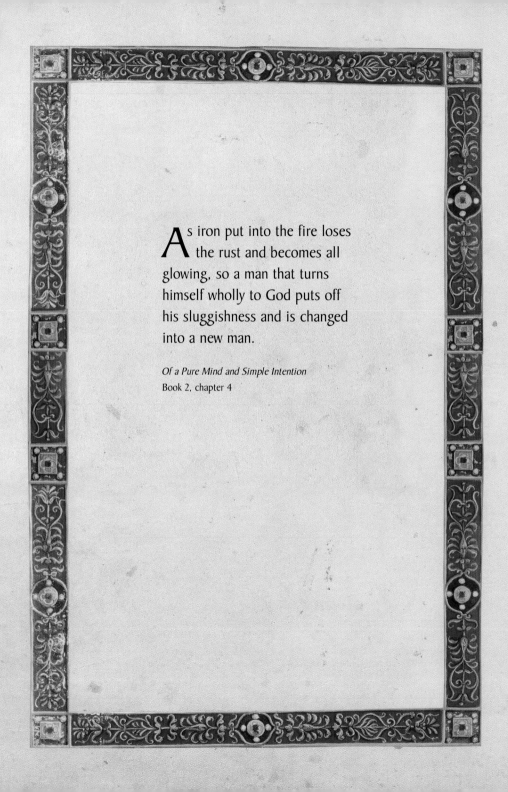

As iron put into the fire loses the rust and becomes all glowing, so a man that turns himself wholly to God puts off his sluggishness and is changed into a new man.

Of a Pure Mind and Simple Intention
Book 2, chapter 4

We cannot trust much to ourselves, because we often want grace and understanding.

There is but little light in us and this we quickly lose through negligence.

Many times also we perceive not that we are so blind interiorly.

We often do ill and do worse in excusing it.

We are sometimes moved with passion, and we mistake it for zeal.

We blame little things in others and pass over great things in ourselves.

We are quick enough at perceiving and weighing what we suffer from others, but we mind not what others suffer from us.

He that would well and duly weigh his own deeds would have no room to judge hardly of others.

Of the Consideration of One's Self
Book 2, chapter 5

He will easily be content and in peace whose conscience is clean.

Thou art not more holy if thou art praised nor anything the worse if thou art dispraised.

What thou art that thou art, nor canst thou be said to be greater than God sees thee to be.

If thou consider well what thou art within thyself thou wilt not care what men say of thee.

Man beholds the face, but God looks upon the heart. Man considers the actions, but God weighs the intentions.

To do always well and to hold one's self in small account is a mark of an humble soul.

To refuse comfort from any created thing is a sign of great purity and interior confidence.

Of the Joy of a Good Conscience
Book 2, chapter 6

Let all things be loved for Jesus' sake,
but Jesus for His own sake.

Jesus Christ alone is singularly to be loved,
who alone is found good and faithful above
all friends.

For His sake, and in Him, let both friends
and enemies be dear to thee, and for all these
thou must pray to Him that all may know and
love Him.

Neither desire to be singularly praised nor
beloved; for this belongs to God alone, who
hath none like to Himself.

Neither desire that anyone's heart should be
set on thee; nor do thou let thyself be taken
up with the love of anyone, but let Jesus be
in thee, and in every good man.

Of Familiar Friendship with Jesus
Book 2, chapter 8

I never found anyone so religious and devout as not to have sometimes a subtraction of grace, or feel a diminution of fervour.

No saint was ever so highly rapt and illuminated as not to be tempted sooner or later.

For he is not worthy of the high contemplation of God who has not, for God's sake, been exercised with some tribulation.

For temptation going before is usually a sign of ensuing consolation.

For heavenly comfort is promised to such as have been proved by temptation. "To him that overcometh," saith Our Lord, "I will give to eat of the tree of life."

Of the Want of All Comforts
Book 2, chapter 9

B e grateful then for the least and thou shalt be worthy to receive greater things.

Let the least be to thee as something very great, and the most contemptible as a special favour.

If thou considerest the dignity of the Giver, no gift will seem to thee little which is given by so great a God.

Yea, though He give punishment and stripes, it ought to be acceptable; for whatever He suffers to befall us, He always does it for our salvation.

He that desires to retain the grace of God let him be thankful for grace when it is given, and patient when it is withdrawn: let him pray that it may return; let him be cautious and humble, lest he lose it.

Of Gratitude for the Grace of God
Book 2, chapter 10

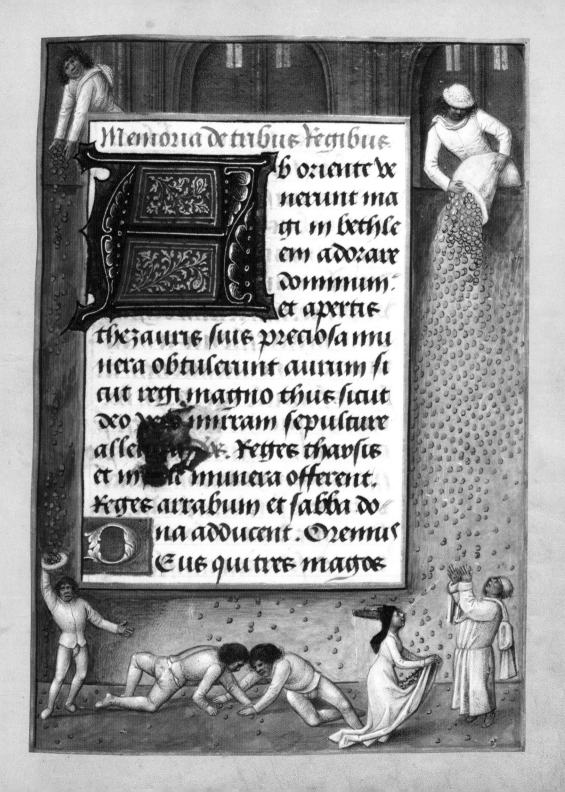

Memoria de tribus regibus.

Ab oriente ve
nerunt ma
gi in bethle
em adorare
dominum.
Et apertis
thezauris suis preciosa mu
nera obtulerunt aurum si
cut regi, magno thus sicut
deo verum miram sepulture
alleluya. R. Reges tharsis
et insule munera offerent.
Reges arrabum et sabba do
na adducent. Oremus
Deus qui tres magos

Oh, how much is the pure love of Jesus able to do when it is not mixed with any self-interest or self-love. Are not all those to be called hirelings who are always seeking consolation?

Are they not proved to be rather lovers of themselves than
of Christ who are always thinking of their own profit and gain?
Where shall we find a man that is willing to serve God gratis?

Of the Small Number of the Lovers of the Cross of Jesus
Book 2, chapter II

Prepare thyself to suffer many adversities and divers evils in this miserable life; for so it will be with thee wherever thou art, and so indeed wilt thou find it wheresoever thou mayest hide thyself.

It must be so, and there is no remedy against the tribulation of evil and sorrow but to bear them patiently.

Drink of the chalice of thy Lord lovingly if thou desire to be His friend and to have part with Him.

Of the Royal Way of the Holy Cross
Book 2, chapter 12

BOOK III
Of Internal Consolation

Love is an excellent thing, a great good indeed, which alone maketh light all that is burdensome and equally bears all that is unequal.

For it carries a burden without being burdened and makes all that which is bitter sweet and savoury.

The love of Jesus is noble and generous; it spurs us on to do great things and excites us to desire always that which is most perfect.

Love will tend upwards and is not to be detained by things beneath.

Love will be at liberty and free from all worldly affections, lest its interior sight be hindered, lest it suffer itself to be entangled with any temporal interest or cast down by losses.

Nothing is sweeter than love; nothing stronger, nothing higher, nothing more generous, nothing more pleasant, nothing fuller or better in Heaven or on earth; for love proceeds from God and cannot rest but in God above all things created.

The Wonderful Effects of Divine Love
Book 3, chapter 5

Love watches, and sleeping, slumbers not.

When weary is not tired; when straitened is not constrained; when frighted is not disturbed, but like a lively flame and a torch all on fire it mounts upwards and securely passes through all opposition.

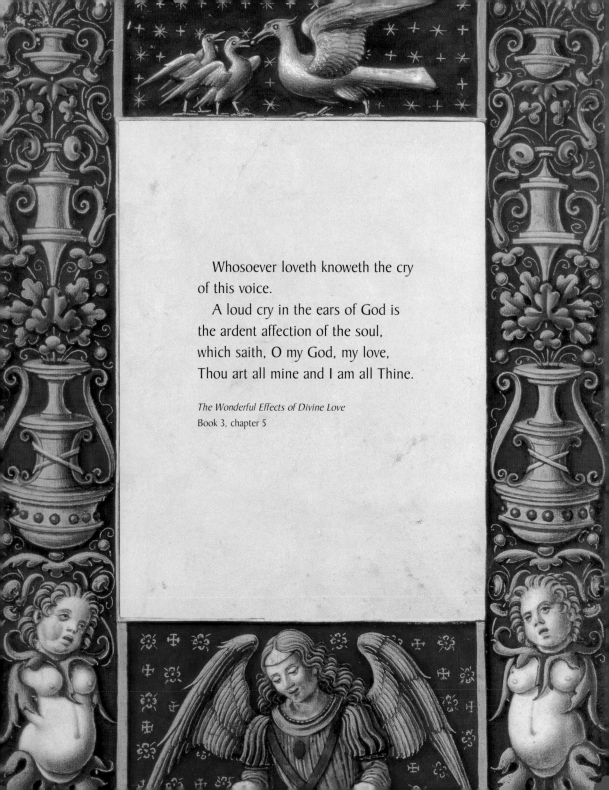

Whosoever loveth knoweth the cry of this voice.

A loud cry in the ears of God is the ardent affection of the soul, which saith, O my God, my love, Thou art all mine and I am all Thine.

The Wonderful Effects of Divine Love
Book 3, chapter 5

Love is swift, sincere, pious, pleasant, and delightful; strong, patient, faithful, prudent, long-suffering, courageous, and never seeking itself.

For where a man seeks himself there he falls from love.

The Wonderful Effects of Divine Love
Book 3, chapter 5

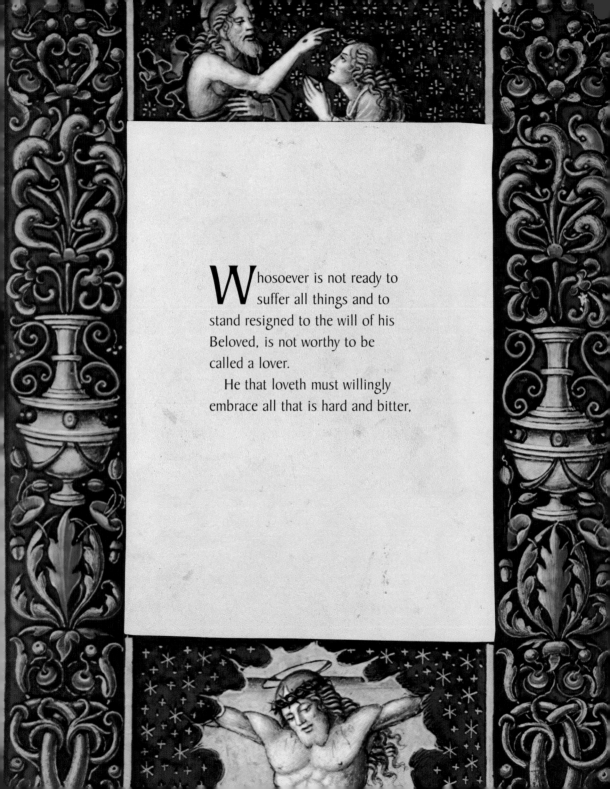

Whosoever is not ready to suffer all things and to stand resigned to the will of his Beloved, is not worthy to be called a lover.

He that loveth must willingly embrace all that is hard and bitter,

for the sake of his Beloved, and never suffer himself to be turned away from Him by any contrary occurrences whatsoever.

The Wonderful Effects of Divine Love
Book 3, chapter 5

W hat shall I give Thee for so many thousands of favours? Oh, that I could serve Thee all the days of my life!

Oh, that I were able, if it were but for one day, to serve Thee worthily!

Indeed Thou art worthy of all service, of all honour, and of eternal praise!

Thou art truly my Lord and I am Thy poor servant, who am bound with all my strength to serve Thee and ought never to grow weary of praising Thee.

This is my will, this is my desire, and whatever is wanting to me do Thou vouchsafe to supply.

It Is Sweet to Serve God, Despising this World
Book 3, chapter 10

If thou shalt say thou art not able to suffer so much, how then wilt thou endure the fire of Purgatory?

Of two evils one ought always to choose the less.

Of Learning Patience, and of Fighting against Concupiscence
Book 3, chapter 12

A las, how many would have stayed afar off and a great way behind, if they had not before their eyes Thine excellent example?

Behold we are still tepid, notwithstanding all Thy miracles and the instructions we have heard: what then would it have been if we had not this great light to follow Thee.

Temporal Miseries are to be Borne with Patience, after the Example of Jesus Christ
Book 3, chapter 18

He is not truly a patient man who will suffer no more than he thinks good and from whom it pleases him.

The truly patient man minds not by whom it is he is exercised, whether by his superior, or by one of his equals, or by an inferior: whether by a good and holy man, or by one that is perverse and unworthy.

But how much soever and how often soever any adversity happens to him from anything created, he takes it all with equality of mind, as from the hand of God, with thanksgiving and esteems it a great gain.

For nothing, how little soever, that is suffered for God's sake, can pass without merit in the sight of God.

On Supporting Injuries, and Who is Proved to be Truly Patient
Book 3, chapter 19

au mardi les heures de tous sains.

Omne labia mea

apries

Et os meum an

nunciabit laudem tuam.

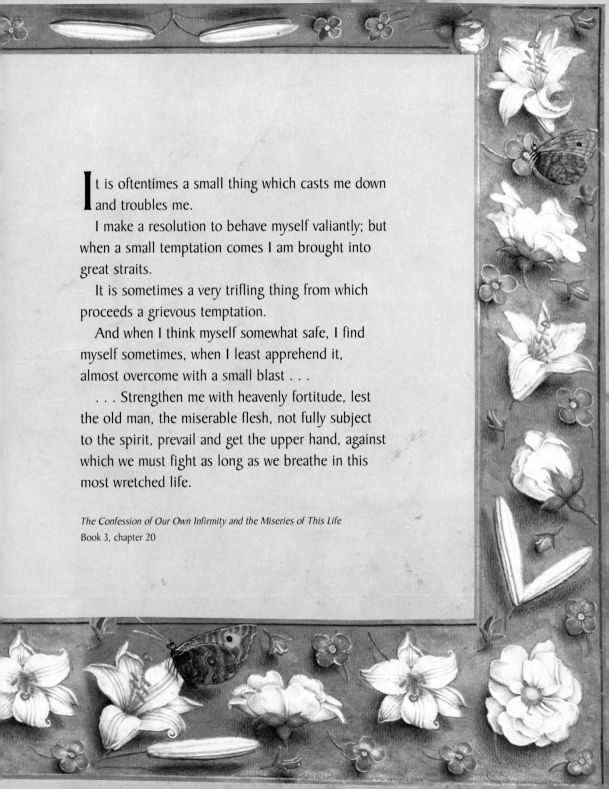

It is oftentimes a small thing which casts me down and troubles me.

I make a resolution to behave myself valiantly; but when a small temptation comes I am brought into great straits.

It is sometimes a very trifling thing from which proceeds a grievous temptation.

And when I think myself somewhat safe, I find myself sometimes, when I least apprehend it, almost overcome with a small blast . . .

. . . Strengthen me with heavenly fortitude, lest the old man, the miserable flesh, not fully subject to the spirit, prevail and get the upper hand, against which we must fight as long as we breathe in this most wretched life.

The Confession of Our Own Infirmity and the Miseries of This Life
Book 3, chapter 20

Send forth Thy light and Thy truth, that they may shine upon the earth; for I am as earth that is empty and void till Thou enlighten me.

Pour forth Thy grace from above, water my heart with the dew of Heaven; send down the waters of devotion to wash the face of this earth, to bring forth good and perfect fruit.

Lift up my mind, oppressed with the load of sins, and raise my whole desires towards heavenly things, that, having tasted the sweetness of the happiness above, I may have no pleasure in thinking of the things of the earth.

Draw me away and deliver me from all unstable comfort of creatures; for no created thing can fully quiet and satisfy my desires.

Join me to Thyself by an inseparable bond of love; for Thou alone canst satisfy the lover, and without Thee all other things are frivolous.

Four Things which Bring Much Peace
Book 3, chapter 23

Who art thou, that thou shouldst be afraid of a mortal man? Today he is, and tomorrow he appears no more.

Fear God, and thou shalt have no need of being afraid of man.

What can anyone do against thee by his words or injuries? He rather hurts himself than thee, nor can he escape the judgment of God whoever he be.

See thou have God before thine eyes and do not contend with complaining words.

And if at present thou seem to be overcome, and to suffer a confusion which thou hast not deserved, do not repine at this and do not lessen thy crown by impatience.

Against the Vain Judgments of Men
Book 3, chapter 36

D o thy part well; mind what thou art about; labour faithfully in My vineyard, I will be thy reward.

Write, read, sing, sigh, keep silence, pray, bear thy crosses manfully; eternal life is worthy of all these, and greater combats.

Peace shall come in one day, which is known to the Lord; and it shall not be a vicissitude of day and night, such as is at present; but everlasting light, infinite brightness, steadfast peace, and secure rest.

Thou shalt not then say: Who shall deliver me from the body of this death? Nor shalt thou cry out: Woe is me, that my sojourning is prolonged. For death shall be no more, but never-failing health; no anxiety, but blessed delight; and a society sweet and lovely.

All Grievous Things are to be Endured for Eternal Life
Book 3, chapter 47

pons + aīe nos defēdas + pſētis̄ vite
ſaluté cōferas + ad gaudia cclox
pducas. P xp̄m dn̄m n̄rm Amē

Narts, no riches, no beauty or strength, no wit or eloquence, are of any worth with Thee, O Lord, without grace.

The Corruption of Nature, and of the Efficacy of Divine Grace
Book 3, chapter 55

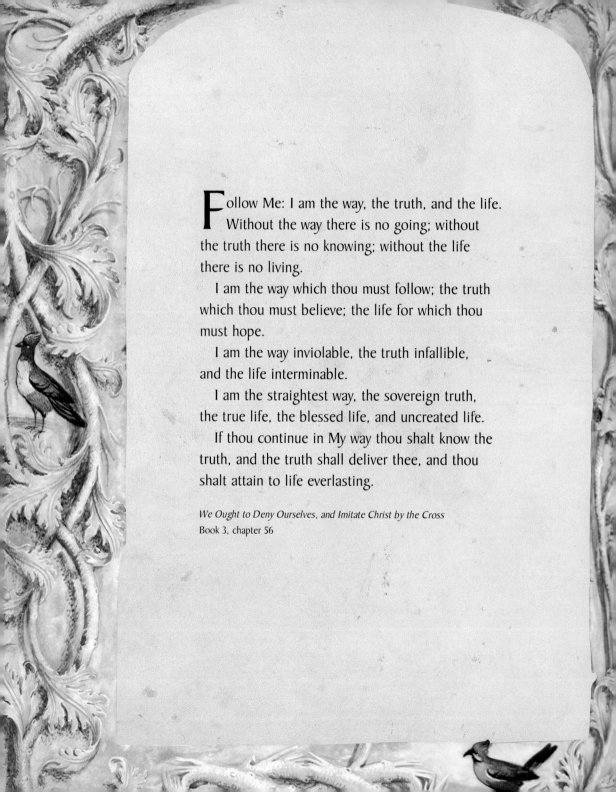

F ollow Me: I am the way, the truth, and the life.
Without the way there is no going; without
the truth there is no knowing; without the life
there is no living.

I am the way which thou must follow; the truth
which thou must believe; the life for which thou
must hope.

I am the way inviolable, the truth infallible,
and the life interminable.

I am the straightest way, the sovereign truth,
the true life, the blessed life, and uncreated life.

If thou continue in My way thou shalt know the
truth, and the truth shall deliver thee, and thou
shalt attain to life everlasting.

We Ought to Deny Ourselves, and Imitate Christ by the Cross
Book 3, chapter 56

In sabbo scō pasche Ad vs Al-
leluia al-
leluia alla
tota diei
turaū ps
Laudate
dūm ōes
Gloria ⁊ repetitaū post psal-
mum sequitur. Ad magnifi-
catanti phona Vespere autē

sabbati qͥ lucescit in pͥma sabbati nenit maria magdalēa
⁊ altera maria uidere sepulcꝛ
alla Dēo magnificat ⁊ ant
repetitur. Dͣs uobiscū
oremus Oratio
Spͥritum nobis ꝺ
domine tue cari-
tatis infunde ut quos sacꝛ
mentis paschalibꝰ satiasti

If thou wilt enter into life, keep the Commandments.
If thou wilt know the truth, believe Me.
If thou wilt be perfect, sell all things.
If thou wilt be My disciple, deny thyself.
If thou wilt possess a blessed life, despise this present life.
If thou wilt be exalted in Heaven, humble thyself in this world.
If thou wilt reign with Me, bear the cross with Me.
For none but the servants of the cross find the way
of bliss and true light.

We Ought to Deny Ourselves, and Imitate Christ by the Cross
Book 3, chapter 56

Woe to those who disdain to humble themselves willingly with little children; for the low gates of the heavenly Kingdom will not suffer them to enter therein.

Of Not Searching into High Matters, nor into the Secret Judgments of God
Book 3, chapter 58

Where was I ever well without Thee? or when could things go ill with me when Thou wast present?

I had rather be poor for Thee than rich without Thee.

I choose rather to sojourn upon earth with Thee than to possess Heaven without Thee. Where Thou art there is Heaven; and there is death and Hell where Thou art not.

All Hope and Confidence is to be Fixed in God Alone
Book 3, chapter 59

BOOK IV

Of the Blessed Sacrament

Offer thyself to Me, and give thy whole self for God, and thine offering will be accepted.

Behold, I offered My whole self to the Father for thee, and have given My whole Body and Blood for thy food, that I might be all thine, and thou mightest be always Mine.

But if thou wilt stand upon thine own self, and wilt not offer thyself freely to My will, thine offering is not perfect, nor will there be an entire union between us.

Therefore, before all thy works, thou must make a free oblation of thyself into the hands of God, if thou desire to obtain liberty and grace.

For the reason why so few become illuminated and internally free is because they do not wholly renounce themselves.

My sentence stands firm: Unless a man renounce all he cannot be my disciple. If, therefore, thou desire to be My disciple, offer up thyself to Me with all thine affections.

Of the Oblation of Christ on the Cross, and of Our Own Resignation
Book 4, chapter 8

Oh, how sweet is Thy spirit, O Lord, Who, to show Thy sweetness towards Thy children, vouchsafest to feed them with the most delicious bread which cometh down from Heaven!

That a Devout Soul Ought to Desire, with her Whole Heart, to be United to Christ in this Sacrament
Book 4, chapter 13

If grace were always presently given, and ever at hand with a wish, it would be more than man's infirmity could well bear.

Therefore the grace of devotion is to be expected with a good hope and humble patience. Yet impute it to thyself and to thy sins, when it is not given thee, or when it is secretly taken away.

It is sometimes a little thing that hinders or hides grace from thee; if that may be called a little, and not rather great, which hindereth so great a good.

But if thou remove this same, be it small or great, and perfectly overcome it, thou shalt have thy desire.

That the Grace of Devotion is Obtained by Humility and Self-Denial
Book 4, chapter 15

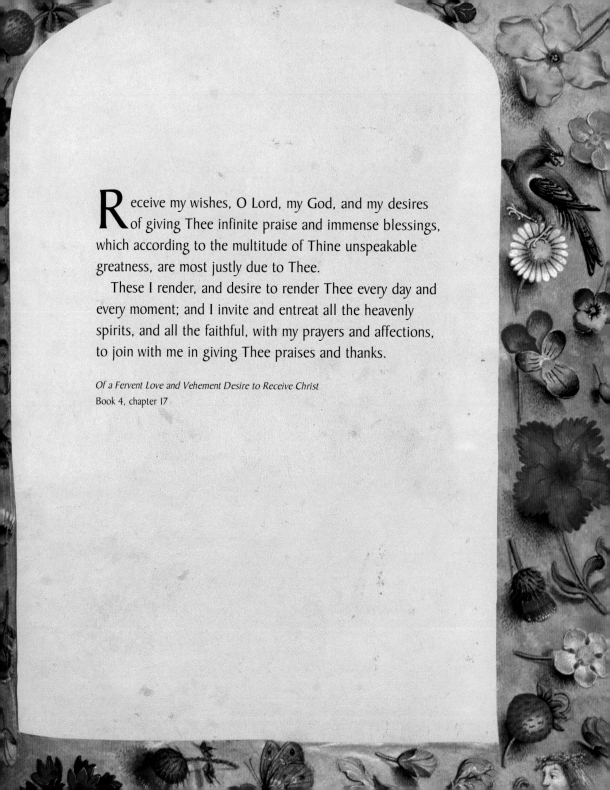

Receive my wishes, O Lord, my God, and my desires of giving Thee infinite praise and immense blessings, which according to the multitude of Thine unspeakable greatness, are most justly due to Thee.

These I render, and desire to render Thee every day and every moment; and I invite and entreat all the heavenly spirits, and all the faithful, with my prayers and affections, to join with me in giving Thee praises and thanks.

Of a Fervent Love and Vehement Desire to Receive Christ
Book 4, chapter 17

In festinitate oñis scor / bentem signum dei vim
ad vñ super ps salmo ajj / r clamauit voce magna
qz glorosu / quatuor angelis quibz
e regnu in / datum est nocere terre r
quo cum xp̃ / mari dicens Nolite no
gaudent oẽs / cere terre r mari neqz ar
scte amicta / boribus: quo adusqz sig
stolis albis / nemus seruos dei nri in
r sequuntur agnum quo / frontibus coꝝ Ꝛ Con
cumqz ient ps: Laudate / cede nr. Hymnus.
pueri Cum ceteris capl̃z / Ihesu saluator
Ecce ego iohẽs / seculi redemptio
vidi alterum / ope subueni r
angelum ascen / pia dei genitrix
dentem ab ortu solis ha / salutem posce miseris

LIST OF ILLUSTRATIONS